Hidden Treasures: Small Businesses Doing Great Things In The Pacific Northwest

Hidden Treasures: Small Businesses Doing Great Things In The Pacific Northwest

Swannee Rivers

iUniverse, Inc.

New York Lincoln Shanghai

Hidden Treasures:
Small Businesses Doing Great Things In The Pacific Northwest

iUniverse books may be ordered through booksellers or by contacting:

iUniverse
2021 Pine Lake Road, Suite 100
Lincoln, NE 68512
www.iuniverse.com
1-800-Authors (1-800-288-4677)

ISBN: 978-0-595-44914-9 (pbk)
ISBN: 978-0-595-89237-2 (ebk)

Printed in the United States of America

I would like to dedicate this directory to the inspirational business women that have entered my life during the past two years. Thank you for your belief, trust, support and commitment as I launched Women's Showcases in the Renton, Washington community. It is because of each of you and the unique talents you have shared and entrusted me to present to others we have been given the opportunity to strengthen. Your presence has become a powerful force synonymous with respect. News of our business network has expanded into outer regions of the Pacific Northwest. I thank each of you for entrusting me to guide you, and applaud those of you that have released fear and began the progression towards business promotion. I am blessed to have the opportunity to share with others the greatness I saw in each of you from the beginning.

To my loving family, husband, James thank you for your support and cheers as I continuously challenge myself, overcome obstacles, and see my dreams become a reality. To my oldest daughter, Patrice what would I do without your support during each showcase? I appreciate all you do. To my baby girl, Paris thank you for helping "momma" always pull things together at the last minute. It is amazing to watch and see how much you already understand about "momma's business stuff." You are all true angels in my eyes.

To the supporters of our showcases, women in business, and small businesses everywhere I thank you. You are the ones that make things happen and continually encourage us to strive for the best, and to be as competitive as we know we can in the business arena.

To the general public, many of you took the time to contact me via email, telephone, and in person to let me know about businesses you felt were worthy of being mentioned in this directory. Your feedback is appreciated, and without it none of this would be possible.

Swannee Rivers

Contents

INTRODUCTION

Why create this business directory? I felt the calling to do so. There is a vacancy in the business arena for small businesses, homebased and other-wise that I call "hidden treasures." The smaller businesses that some people don't recognize by name but many feel are worthy of being shared with a wider audience. They deserve to be put in a format for all to see. Their turn for attention and applause is long overdue. I knew I was in a position to make this a reality for many.

With twenty plus years in the business world, ten of those years as a part-time homebased business owner I set out on a new venture in 2005. After noting a visible void while discussing business with female acquaintances that were running their own homebased businesses, I wanted to help create publicity for others. Many business owners felt they were not as recognized or respected as the large national chains. Upon closer observation there definitely was no shortage in talent. In some cases I felt the small vendor could run parallel to the large chain products if put to the test. It was at that moment I realized something had to be done, and thus the Women's Showcase of Renton, Washington was born.

For two years monthly business showcases I have developed and organized have been held at the Renton Community Center. It is an opportunity for women who want to promote their business, talent, distribute business cards ... to do so. This "safe environment" has grown in to a respected forum for women wanting to network with others and grow their business. During the past two years I have been given the opportunity to learn, grow and network with hundreds of women and small business owners male and female from various areas of the Pacific Northwest. We have had discussions and exchanged information about what causes some businesses to fail and what qualities contribute to the flourishing of others. I have united women and given them the opportunity to expand beyond the introduction of these showcases. I have learned so much from each individual that has crossed my path. It has been a rewarding accomplishment.

As I collected information from businesses within various communities about others they respected in the industry I knew it was important to share this information. How could others support these businesses if they were not aware of their existence? This is where I knew I could play a major role, and bring about a change.

Swannee Rivers

AUTHOR'S NOTES

This directory has been created solely for informational purposes. After polling hundreds of individuals these businesses have been identified by the general public as ones worthy of mention and recognition by the example they set in the business arena, products distributed through their business, and methods used to conduct business. Some businesses may maintain more than one location, but the location noted for superior business transactions with clientele has been recognized. This directory in no way intends to discredit or tarnish the image of additional locations, or businesses providing similar services. I also have no expectations for you to replace my opinion or those shared by others for your own. It is my hope that each buyer of this directory will learn of a new business in their community and surrounding areas and learn the true value of small businesses in the Pacific Northwest.

ACCOUNTING

Business Name: AC^2- Accounting & Computing Consultants   RENTON
Owner(s): Darryl Corfman
Business Established in: 1990
Business Telephone Number: (253) 951-8759
Business Contact email address: darryl@corfman.com

Hours of Operation: Monday-Friday 9:00am-3:00pm by appointment only

This dynamic small business has been a well respected establishment within the Renton community for many years. With a vast array of experience AC^2 specializes in small business accounting, and is able to assist business owners by demonstrating proper accounting techniques and simplified organizational systems to conduct their business affairs. Customers receive individual assistance which makes for a pleasant business experience. Cash or checks are acceptable forms of payment.

Business Name: A to Z Tax Service   RENTON
                111 Factory N.
                Renton, WA. 98057

Business Telephone Number: (425) 228-6519

APPLIANCES

Business Name: King and Bunny's   RENTON
                        4608 NE. Sunset Blvd.
                        Renton, WA. 98059

Business Telephone Number: (425) 277-0600
Business Website: www.kingandbunnys.com

Business Name: Jack Roberts Appliance   TACOMA
                        5049 So. Tacoma Way
                        Tacoma, WA. 98409

Business Telephone Number: (253) 475-4088

Business Name: Albert Lee Appliance   TUKWILA
                        404 Strander Blvd.
                        Tukwila, WA. 98188

Business Telephone Number: (206) 433-1110

Business Name: Appliance Master   BUCKLEY
                        8513 272nd Ave. E.
                        Buckley, WA. 98321

Business Telephone Number: (360) 825-2084

Business Name: Dave's Appliance Rebuild   SEATTLE
                        1505 E. Pine St.
                        Seattle, WA. 98122

Business Telephone Number: (206) 324-3270

Business Name: Frederick's Appliance   REDMOND
16109 Redmond Way
Redmond, WA. 98052

Business Telephone Number: (425) 885-0000
1(866) 309-3767
Business Website: www.fredericksappliance.com

Business Name: Lucky Brush Heart and Home   PUYALLUP
14104 Meridian E.
Puyallup, WA. 98373

Business Telephone Number: (253) 848-9959
Business Website: www.luckybrush.com

AUTHORS

Business Name: Swannee Rivers Literary and Referral Agency   RENTON
Owner(s): Swannee Rivers
Business Established in: 1999
Business Telephone Number: (425) 277-2950
Business Contact Email address: swanneerivers@mindspring.com
Business Website: www.swanneerivers.com

Hours of Operation: Monday-Friday 9:00-5:30pm

In 2004 Swannee Rivers burst into the writing arena with a vengeance. Her literary work
Healthcare Under Duress: An Inside look at the University of Washington Billing Scandal presents one woman's personal account and experience within a prestigious University Hospital (UWP).

This case is unique, representing the issuance of the largest fine ever given to a medical teaching institution within the United States for billing fraud.

For years, Swannee Rivers maintained hope of one day seeing justice served. In 2000 the FBI arrived, giving her that opportunity.

Never one to succumb to obstacles her proceeding works, journals, tackled everyday issues many were hesitant to address: *Cancer Journal for the Survivor in You, Parent's Don't Know Everything: A Teen Freedom of Expression Journal.* Check out her website to learn more about potential freelance writing opportunities with this author.

ARTISTS

Business Name: Watercolors by Pat Lambert   AUBURN

Business Email address: pats.watercolors@yahoo.com

This talented artist has many years of painting experience under her belt. Known for her original pieces of artwork throughout the Pacific Northwest, Pat has always had a love for creativity and sharing. Pat offers: Original Paintings, and has the ability to paint MEMORIES from your 4x5 or 4x6 color photograph, wedding picture, portrait, special place you have visited or perhaps the last trip you shared with that special someone in your life. She also features: Gicleé-Prints of Originals

11x14 or 8x10 matted only or matted and framed

5x7 blank cards (print on the front)/Magnets

Color brochure available upon request/Quantity discounts

BAKERS/BAKERIES

Business Name: Great Harvest Bread Company   BELLEVUE
                3610 Factoria Blvd. SE.
                Bellevue, WA. 98006

Business Telephone Number: (425) 643-8420

Business Name: Sharon's Catering and Cakes   BELLEVUE
                6105 125th Ave. SE.
                Bellevue, WA. 98006

Business Telephone Number: (425) 747-3018

Business Name: The Australian Pie Company   BURIEN
                425 SW.152nd St.
                Burien, WA. 98166

Business Telephone Number: (206) 243-4138

Business Name: Geno's Coffee Shop and Bakery   BURIEN
                11620 Ambaum Blvd.
                Burien, WA. 98146

Business Telephone Number: (206) 244-4303

Business Name: Delit Bakery   SEATTLE
                2701 15th Ave. S.
                Seattle, WA. 98144

Business Telephone Number: (206) 325-2114

Business Name: Borracchini's Bakery and Mediterranean Market SEATTLE
2307 Rainier Ave. S.
Seattle, WA. 98144

Business Telephone Number: (206) 325-1550

Business Name: Honey Bear Bakery SEATTLE
6504 20th NE.
Seattle, WA. 98115

Business Telephone Number: (206) 525-2790

Business Name: Simply Desserts SEATTLE
3421 Fremont Ave. N.
Seattle, WA. 98103

Business Telephone Number: (206) 633-2671

Business Name: Top Pot Capitol Hill SEATTLE
609 Summit Ave. E.
Seattle, WA. 98102

Business Telephone Number: (206) 323-7841
Business Website: www.toppotdonuts.com

Business Name: Taste Good Bakery RENTON
229 S. 4th Pl
Renton, WA. 98055

Business Telephone Number: (425) 204-9331

Business Name: Gais Northwest Bakery TUKWILA
17500 W. Valley Highway
Tukwila, WA. 98188

Business Telephone Number: (425) 251-0431

Business Name: Creative Cake Designs   KENT
                20855 108th Ave. SE.
                Kent, WA. 98031

Business Telephone Number: (253) 859-2812

Business Name: Simply Delicious Cake Bakery   KENT
                21224 84th Ave. S.
                Kent, WA. 98032

Business Telephone Number: (253) 395-5572

Business Name: Bakery Express   KENT
                10214 SE. 240th
                Kent, WA. 98031

Business Telephone Number: (253) 850-2827

Business Name: An Xuyen Bakery   SEATAC
                2823 S. 200th St.
                Seatac, WA. 98198

Business Telephone Number: (206) 878-4086

Business Name: Pioneer Bakery and Coffee Shop   PUYALLUP
                120 S. Meridian
                Puyallup, WA. 98371

Business Telephone Number: (253) 845-8336

Business Name: Hoffman's Fine Cakes and Pastries   KIRKLAND
                226 Parkplace Ctr.
                Kirkland, WA. 98033

Business Telephone Number: (425) 828-0926
Business Website: www.hoffmansfinepastries.com

Business Name: Hancock's Bakery   REDMOND
                16150 NE 85th St.
                Redmond, WA. 98052

Business Telephone Number: (425)885-3780

BEAUTY

Business Name: Salon Totality KENT
841 North Central Avenue, Suite C-109
Kent, WA. 98032

Business Telephone Number: (253) 856-1638

Salon Totality maintains the goal of providing the best customer service and appreciation to all their customers. Complimentary consultations are offered for all services. Customers are also welcome to complimentary bangs and neck trims. Great discounts are offered with the salons pre-book/pre-pay system that ensures desired weekly and bi-weekly standing appointments. Salon Totality caters to all hair types.

Business Name: Aaina Beauty Salon KENT
24616 Military Rd.
Kent, WA. 98032

Business Telephone Number: (253) 946-0105

Business Name: Kathy's Hair Design KENT
25403 104th SE
Kent, WA. 98030

Business Telephone Number: (253) 852-1069

Business Name: International Look Beauty Salon KENT
25614 Pacific Highway So.
Kent, WA. 98032

Business Telephone Number: (253) 839-1881

Business Name: Guys and Gals Hair Design   FEDERAL WAY
                29005 Pacific Highway So.
                Federal Way, WA. 98003

Business Telephone Number: (253) 839-0667

Business Name: Hair Creations   FEDERAL WAY
                2319 SW 336th
                Federal Way, WA. 98023

Business Telephone Number: (253) 874-8371

Business Name: MOA   FEDERAL WAY
                2020 S. 320th St. Bldg. H
                Federal Way, WA. 98003

Business Telephone Number: (253) 941-8922

Business Name: Impressions Full Service Salon and Spa   RENTON
                17650 140th Ave SE
                Renton, WA. 98058

Business Telephone Number: (425) 226-6560

Business Name: Sharon's Shear Delight Styling Salon, Inc.   RENTON
                334 Well Ave, S. Ste. A
                Renton, WA. 98057

Business Telephone Number: (425) 227-8057

Business Name: Oasis Skin and Nails Day Spa and Massage Clinic RENTON
                 10712 SE. Carr Road
                 Renton, WA. 98055

Business Telephone Number: (425) 282-5046

Business Name: Beauty Wave   RENTON
                18665 108th Ave. SE.
                Renton, WA. 98055

Business Telephone Number (425) 226-8811

Business Name: Boulevard Salon   RENTON
                3212 Lake Washington Blvd. N
                Renton, WA. 98056

Business Telephone Number: (425) 255-1064

Business Name: Angel Nails   RENTON
                20 SW. 7th Ste. D
                Renton, WA. 98057

Business Telephone Number: (425) 793-5063

Business Name: First Nails   RENTON
                1200 Bronson Way N.
                Renton, WA. 98055

Business Telephone Number: (425) 917-0988

Business Name: Cascade Beauty College LLC   RENTON
                17060 116th Avenue SE.
                Renton, WA. 98058

Business Telephone Number: (425) 226-2457

Business Name: Euro Institute of Skin Care   RENTON
                10904 SE. 176th Street
                Renton, WA. 98055

Business Telephone Number: (425) 255-8100

Business Name: Peace and Tranquility Day Spa and Massage   RENTON
518 S. Tobin St.
Renton, WA. 98057

Business Telephone Number: (206) 715-9027

Business Name: BJ Beauty Supplies   RENTON
321 S. 2nd
Renton, WA. 98057

Business Telephone Number: (425) 255-0778

Business Name: Natural Nails   KENT
3168 NE. Sunset Blvd.
Renton, WA. 98056

Business Telephone Number: (425) 235-6133

Business Name: Kathy Nails   KENT
418 W. Meeker
Kent, WA. 98032

Business Telephone Number: (253) 859-1399

Business Name: Lovely Nails   KENT
429 E. Smith St.
Kent, WA. 98032

Business Telephone Number: (253) 850-3169

Business Name: Daniel Ross Salon and Skincare   COVINGTON
16915 SE 272nd St.
Covington, WA. 98042

Business Telephone Number: (253) 630-9423

Business Name: Hair Scene   COVINGTON
                16204 SE. 272nd
                Covington, WA. 98042

Business Telephone Number: (253) 638-0225

Business Name: Nail Genie   COVINGTON
                30211 176th Ave. SE.
                Covington, WA. 98042

Business Telephone Number: (253) 630-4362

Business Name: Covington Nail   COVINGTON
                17051 SE. 272nd St.
                Covington, WA. 98042

Business Telephone Number: (253) 630-3775

Business Name: London House Full Service Salon   BURIEN
                13028 1st Ave. S.
                Burien, WA. 98168

Business Telephone Number: (206) 2443006
Business Website: www.londonhousesalon.com

Business Name: Burien Nail and Spa   BURIEN
                15004 Ambaum Blvd. SW.
                Burien, WA. 98166

Business Telephone Number: (206) 988-0520

Business Name: Star Nails   BURIEN
                14259 Ambaum Blvd. SW.
                Burien, WA. 98166

Business Telephone Number: (206) 241-6166

Business Name: Just Another Salon   SUMNER
                909 Alder Avenue
                Sumner, WA. 98390

Business Telephone Number: (253) 891-3611

Business Name: Nail Center   SUMNER
                15105 Main St. E.
                Sumner, WA. 98390

Business Telephone Number: (253) 863-4051

Business Name: Shear Magic Salon   BUCKLEY
                912 Main St.
                Buckley, WA. 98321

Business Telephone Number: (253) 829-0322

Business Name: Sandra's Beauty Salon   PUYALLUP
                615 E. Main Ave.
                Puyallup, WA. 98372

Business Telephone Number: (253) 848-2900

Business Name: In Style Salon   PUYALLUP
                702 S. Hill Park DR.
                Puyallup, WA. 98373

Business Telephone Number: (253)770-3744

Business Name: Kristine's Styling Salon   PUYALLUP
                109 W. Meeker
                Puyallup, WA. 98371

Business Telephone Number: (253) 845-1101

Business Name: Madison's   PUYALLUP
                10124 18th St. Ct. E.
                Puyallup, WA. 98371

Business Telephone Number: (253) 927-3980

Business Name: Salon Escape   PUYALLUP
                17530 Meridian E.
                Puyallup, WA. 98375

Business Telephone Number: (253) 840-6062

Business Name: Salon Image   QUEEN ANNE
                621 Queen Anne Avenue N.
                Seattle, WA. 98109

Business Telephone Number: (206) 283-2611

Business Name: Elegant Touch   EVERETT
                8604 9th Ave. SE.
                Everett, WA. 98208

Business Telephone Number: (425) 438-1267

Business Name: Adair's Hair Salon   SNOHOMISH
                127 Avenue A #A
                Snohomish, WA. 98290

Business Telephone Number: (360) 568-5233

Business Name: Aphrodite Salon   SNOHOMISH
                511 Maple Avenue
                Snohomish, WA. 98290

Business Telephone Number: (360) 563-9455
Business Website: www.aphroditehairsalon.com

Business Name: Awesome Nail and Hair   SNOHOMISH
                813 Avenue D
                Snohomish, WA. 98290

Business Telephone Number: (360) 568-4701

Business Name: Angel Haircut   SNOHOMISH
                3922 148th St. SE.
                Snohomish, WA. 98296

Business Telephone Number: (425) 357-1847

Business Name: DeCharlenes Beauty Shop and Boutique   SEATTLE
                2801 E. Madison
                Seattle, WA. 98112

Business Telephone Number: (206) 322-8296

Business Name: Liana Hair Salon   SEATTLE
                1125 E. Olive Street
                Seattle, WA. 98122

Business Telephone Number: (206) 860-4835

Business Name: Vogue Coiffure Beauty Salon   SEATTLE
1108 23rd Avenue
Seattle, WA. 98122

Business Telephone Number: (206) 323-6551

Business Name: The Hair Connection   SEATTLE
321 Broadway E.
Seattle, WA. 98102

Business Telephone Number: (206) 323-1211

Business Name: Update Barber Shop and Beauty Salon   SEATTLE
701 23rd Avenue
Seattle, WA. 98122

Business Telephone Number: (206) 860-8560

Business Name: USA Nails   SEATTLE
1721 22nd Avenue
Seattle, WA. 98122

Business Telephone Number: (206) 329-4273

Business Name: Mid K Beauty Supply   SEATTLE
6032 Martin Luther King Jr. Way
Seattle, WA. 98118

Business Telephone Number: (206) 723-6714

Business Name: Mid K Beauty Supply   SEATTLE
5620 Rainier Avenue South
Seattle, WA. 98118

Business Telephone Number: (206) 723-3643

Business Name: Salon Lorache   SEATTLE
               4901 Rainier Avenue So.
               Seattle, WA. 98118

Business Telephone Number: (206) 722-0371

BOOKSTORES

Business Name: Bookworm Exchange   SEATTLE
                4860 Rainier Avenue So.
                Seattle, WA. 98118

Business Telephone Number: (206) 722-6633

Business Name: Bailey Coy Books   SEATTLE
                414 Broadway E.
                Seattle, WA. 98102

Business Telephone Number: (206) 323-8842

Business Name: Elliot Bay Book Company   SEATTLE
                101 S. Main Street
                Seattle, WA. 98104

Business Telephone Number: (206) 624-6600
Business Website: www.elliotbaybook.com

Business Name: Burien Books   BURIEN
                643 SW 152nd St. Ste A
                Burien, WA. 98166

Business Telephone Number: (206) 244-1422

Business Name: Children's Bookshop and Teaching Supplies   BURIEN
                152 SW 152nd St.
                Burien, WA. 98166

Business Telephone Number: (206) 242-9790

Business Name: Howell Religious Gifts and Books   KENT
201 First Avenue So.
Kent, WA. 98032

Business Telephone Number: (253) 520-0695

Business Name: Island Books   MERCER ISLAND
3014 78th Ave. SE.
Mercer Island, WA. 98040

Business Telephone Number: (206) 232-6920
Business Website: www.mercerislandbooks.com

Business Name: Maple Leaf Book Exchange   ISSAQUAH
88 Front St. S.
Issaquah, WA. 98027

Business Telephone Number: (425) 391-0686

Business Name: New Woman Books   KENT
213 W. Meeker Street
Kent, WA. 98032

Business Telephone Number: (253) 854-4311

Business Name: Christian Supply   KENT
316 Washington Ave. S.
Kent, WA. 98032

Business Telephone Number: (253) 852-3600
Business Website: www.christiansupply.net

Business Name: Third Place Books   LAKE FOREST PARK
                17171 Bothell Way NE.
                Lake Forest, WA. 98155

Business Telephone Number: (206) 366-3333
Business Website: www.thirdplacebooks.com

Business Name: Kings Books   TACOMA
                218 St. Helen Avenue
                Tacoma, WA 98402

Business Telephone Number: (253) 272-8801

Business Name: The Comic Den   RENTON
                234 Wells Ave. S.
                Renton, WA. 98057

Business Telephone Number: (425) 235-1663

Business Name: Salt Shaker Christian Book Store   ENUMCLAW
                1216 Initial Avenue
                Enumclaw, WA. 98022

Business Telephone Number: (360) 825-7258

CATERING

Business Name: Ingallina's Box Lunch   SEATTLE
Owner(s): Chris Ingallina
Business Established in: 1991
Business Telephone Number: (206) 766-9400 or 1(866) 766-9400
Business Website: www.ingallina.com
Business Address: 135 S. Lucile Street
                  Seattle, WA. 98018

Hours of Operation: Delivery hours Monday-Friday 6:00am-5pm, Saturday 7am-2pm

Located in the heart of Georgetown this catering shop provides free delivery from Everett to Tacoma. Ingallina's has become widely recognized for its high quality products, beautiful food presentations, and timely delivery. Offering boxed lunches, party platters and gift baskets this company features goods fitting of any budget. Occasional same day delivery available with internet orders placed prior to 9:15am. Ingallina's accepts cash, check, and all major credit cards.

CLOTHING

Business Name: Jockey Person to Person®, Independent Comfort Specialist

AUBURN

Business Owner(s): Zita McLaughlin
Business Telephone Number: (253) 939-7268
(253) 350-6389

Business Website: www.jockeypersontoperson.com

"Jockey Person to Person® offers a stylish line of comfort clothes from one of the worlds most trusted brands. We're starting a comfort revolution with amazing new products sold exclusively through home parties." Cash, major credit cards and personal checks accepted. To learn more about this fabulous line of products, call Zita.

Business Name: Frivolous Boutique   MAPLE VALLEY
                23745 225th Way SE
                Maple Valley, WA. 98038

Business Telephone Number: (425) 413-2055
Business Website: www.shopfrivolous.com

Business Name: Linda's   KENT
                12916 SE Kent Kangley Rd.
                Kent, WA. 98042

Business Telephone Number: (253) 850-4153

Business Name: Avenue   RENTON
                601 S. Grady Way
                Renton, WA. 98055

Business Telephone Number: (425) 228-7827

COFFEE/TEAS SHOPS

Business Name: Bronson Bigfoot Java   RENTON
                      1408 Bronson Ave. N.
                      Renton, WA. 98055

Business Telephone Number: (425) 271-5946

Business Name: Heather's Coffee Shop   RENTON
                      19044 108th Ave. SE. #1
                      Renton, WA. 98055

Business Telephone Number: (425) 254-3456

Business Name: Common Ground Coffee and Cupcakes   RENTON
Business Address: 900 So. 3rd St.
                      Renton, WA. 98057

Business Telephone Number: (425) 235-1717

Business Name: Jet City Espresso   RENTON
                      207 Main Ave. So.
                      Renton, WA. 98055

Business Telephone Number: (425) 235-1529

Business Name: Cedar River Espresso   RENTON
                      16402 Se. 128th
                      Renton, WA. 98059

Business Telephone Number: (425) 430-1266

Business Name: Sorrento's Coffee   RENTON
5325 NE. 4th
Renton, WA. 98056

Business Telephone Number: (425) 228-2951

Business Name: Bella Coffee   RENTON
175 Rainier Avenue
Renton, WA. 98057

Business Telephone Number: (425) 277-5094

Business Name: Espresso Lane   RENTON
10700 SE Carr Rd.
Renton, WA. 98055

Business Telephone Number: (425) 255-6440

Business Name: Blue Dog Coffee House   SEATTLE
5509 University Way NE.
Seattle, WA. 98105

Business Telephone Number: (206) 523-1933

Business Name: Diva Expresso   SEATTLE
8014 Lake City Way NE.
Seattle, WA. 98115

Business Telephone Number: (206) 525-5920

Business Name: Café Allegro Espresso Bar   SEATTLE
4214 University Way NE.
Seattle, WA. 98105

Business Telephone Number: (206) 633-3030

Business Name: Café Bambino   SEATTLE
                405 NW 65th St.
                Seattle, WA. 98117

Business Telephone Number: (206) 633-3030

Business Name: Dragonfly Espresso   EVERETT
                4034 Hoyt Avenue
                Everett, WA. 98201

Business Telephone Number: (425) 374-0848

Business Name: Sara's Coffee Shop   KENT
                212 Central Avenue N
                Kent, WA. 98032

Business Telephone Number: (253) 854-1031

Business Name: Bigfoot Java Espresso   KENT
                21110 84th Avenue So.
                Kent, WA. 98032

Business Telephone Number: (253) 437-1405

Business Name: Caveman Coffee   PUYALLUP
                13003 Canyon Rd. E
                Puyallup, WA. 98373

Business Telephone: (253) 536-3707

Business Name: Associated Espresso   SUMNER
                3819 142nd Ave. E.
                Sumner, WA. 98390

Business Telephone Number: (253) 891-1973

Business Name: Donel's Espresso Service   AUBURN
                1414 A. St. SE.
                Auburn, WA. 98002

Business Telephone Number: (253) 351-0220

Business Name: DeSheri Espresso   BUCKLEY
                192 4th St.
                Buckley, WA. 98321

Business Telephone Number: (360) 829-6318

Business Name: Jidder Bugz   BUCKLEY
                10109 234th Ave. E.
                Buckley, WA. 98321

Business Telephone Number: (253) 891-9818

DRY CLEANERS/LAUNDRIES

Business Name: Personality Cleaners   BURIEN
                13634 1st Ave. S.
                Burien, WA. 98168

Business Telephone Number: (206) 243-3200

Business Name: Vibra Clean   BURIEN
                15006 Ambaum Blvd. SW
                Burien, WA. 98166

Business Telephone Number: (206) 246-9010

Business Name: A/T Laundrey   BURIEN
                15724 1st Ave. S.
                Burien, WA. 98148

Business Telephone Number: (206) 835-2110

Business Name: Burien Laundry   BURIEN
                14300 1st Ave. S.
                Burien, WA. 98168

Business Telephone Number: (206) 248-3770

Business Name: Seattle's Nicest Laundry   BURIEN
                13613 Ambaum Blvd.SW.
                Burien, WA. 98166

Business Telephone Number: (206) 277-7111

Business Name: Taylor's Fine Cleaning   KENT
10441 SE 240th
Kent, WA. 98031

Business Telephone Number: (253) 859-1559

Business Name: Darcie's Laundry   KENT
25664 104th Ave. SE.
Kent, WA. 98030

Business Telephone Number: (253) 850-1986

Business Name: East Hill Cleaners   KENT
25807 104th SE
Kent, WA. 98030

Business Telephone Number: (253) 852-4700

Business Name: Lake Meridian Cleaners   KENT
15220 SE 272nd St. Ste. J
Kent, WA. 98042

Business Telephone Number: (253) 630-2933

Business Name: East Hill Homestyle Laundry   KENT
25631 104th Ave. SE.
Kent, WA. 98030

Business Telephone Number: (253) 852-5850

Business Name: Savanh Laundry   KENT
12960 SE. Kent Kangley Rd.
Kent, WA. 98030

Business Telephone Number: (253) 631-9501

Business Name: DC Laundry   KENT
                          26030 Pacific Highway S.
                          Kent, WA. 98032

Business Telephone Number: (253) 529-0840

Business Name: Best Laundromat   KENT
                          23839 108th SE.
                          Kent, WA. 98031

Business Telephone Number: (253) 850-6222

Business Name: Seward Park Cleaners and Tailors   SEATTLE
                          5017 S. Dawson St.
                          Seattle, WA. 98118

Business Telephone Number: (206) 723-2313

Business Name: Downtown Cleaners and Alterations   SEATTLE
                          703 Madison St.
                          Seattle, WA. 98104

Business Telephone Number: (206) 622-1118

Business Name: Madison Cleaners   SEATTLE
                          2737 E. Madison St.
                          Seattle, WA. 98112

Business Telephone Number: (206) 720- 1569

Business Name: Wardrobe Cleaners   SEATTLE
                          4500 Fauntleroy Way SW.
                          Seattle, WA. 98126

Business Telephone Number: (206) 932-0345

Business Name: Clampitt's Cleaners   ISSAQUAH
                1480 NW Gilman Blvd.
                Issaquah, WA. 98027

Business Telephone Number: (425) 392-7818

Business Name: Captains Cleaners   ISSAQUAH
                1025 NW Gilman Blvd.
                Issaquah, WA. 98027

Business Telephone Number: (425) 391-3643

Business Name: Best Campus Cleaners   FEDERAL WAY
                1907 SW Campus Dr.
                Federal Way, WA. 98023

Business Telephone Number (253) 874-4366

Business Name: The Suds Work   FEDERAL WAY
                1642 SW. Dash Point Rd.
                Federal Way, WA. 98023

Business Telephone Number: (253) 874-0510

Business Name: Redondo Laundromat   FEDERAL WAY
                27211 Pacific Highway S.
                Federal Way, WA. 98003

Business Telephone Number: (253) 946-4319

Business Name: Norge Village Laundromat   FEDERAL WAY
                1905 SW. Campus Drive
                Federal Way, WA. 98023

Business Telephone Number: (253) 874-9603

Business Name: Cascade Cleaners   RENTON
                16912 116th Ave. SE.
                Renton, WA. 98058

Business Telephone Number: (425) 226-2580

Business Name: Mac's 1 Hour Cleaners   RENTON
               10825 SE 176th St.
               Renton, WA. 98055

Business Telephone Number: (425) 228-2190

Business Name: Dry Clean Doctor   RENTON
                10736 SE Carr Rd.
                Renton, WA. 98055

Business Telephone Number: (425) 430-9481

Business Name: Fairwood Cleaners   RENTON
                17240 104th SE.
                Renton, WA. 98058

Business Telephone Number: (425) 228-3830

Business Name: Bright and Bold Coin Laundry   RENTON
                3901 NE. 4th St.
                Renton, WA. 98056

Business Telephone: (425) 277-8703

Business Name: Sunshine Wash/Dry Coin-op Laundry   RENTON
                927 Harrington Ave. NE.
                Renton, WA. 98056

Business Telephone Number: (425) 271-5612

Business Name: Wash/Shop   RENTON
17923 108th Ave. SE.
Renton, WA. 98055

Business Telephone Number: (425) 227-6450

Business Name: Vu Laundry   RENTON
1222 Bronson Way N. Ste. 195
Renton, WA. 98055

Business Telephone Number: (425) 235-2312

Business Name: Enumclaw Cleaners   ENUMCLAW
1040 Stevenson
Enumclaw, WA. 98022

Business Telephone Number: (360) 825-8919

Business Name: Grace Cleaners   MAPLE VALLEY
27002 Maple Valley-Black Diamond Rd. SE
Maple Valley, WA. 98038

Business Telephone Number: (425) 432-2155

Business Name: Laundromat Maple Valley Lake Wilderness   MAPLE VALLEY
23714 222nd Pl. SE.
Maple Valley, WA. 98038

Business Telephone Number: (425) 432-6351

Business Name: Down Home Laundry   AUBURN
2826 Auburn Way N.
Auburn, WA. 98002

Business Telephone Number: (253) 735-5216

Business Name: Bakker's Dry Cleaning   KIRKLAND
              11630 98th Ave. NE.
              Kirkland, WA. 98034

Business Telephone Number: (425) 820-1132

Business Name: Overlake Cleaners   REDMOND
              15129 NE. 24th
              Redmond, WA. 98052

Business Telephone Number: (425) 746-7070

EMBROIDERY

Business Name: MelRose Embroidery   BELLEVUE
Business Owner(s) Mel and Rosie McDaniel
Business Established in: 2000
Business Email address: mel_rose@comcast.net

This dynamic small business specializes in custom embroidery for all the special times in life: Weddings, birthdays, holidays, children and grandchildren. Personalized baseball caps, bed, bath and kitchen linens are just the start. No order is too small. Cash, local checks, money orders or cashier check.

Business Name: Bellevue Embroidery   BELLEVUE
                827 Bellevue Way NE
                Bellevue, WA. 98004

Business Telephone Number: (425) 646-9191
Business Website: www.bellevueembroidery.com

Business Name: Stitch Rite Embroidery   SEATTLE
                220 S. Brandon St.
                Seattle, WA. 98118

Business Telephone Number: (206) 766-9958

FLORIST/NURSERIES

Business Name: Painted Tulip Floral Design   RENTON
Business Owner: Darcie Pinz
Business Established in: 2006
Business Address: 401 Olympia Ave. NE.
Business Telephone Number: (425) 687-0933
Business Website: www.paintedtulipfloral.net

Hours of Operation: Monday-Thursday 9:00am-6:00pm
                           Friday 9:00am-7:00pm
                           Saturday 9:00am-5:00pm
                           Sunday by appointment

This emerging new business located in beautiful Renton, Washington has a gift suitable for any event and budget. Specializing in floral arrangements, specialty gifts, weddings, funerals, houseplants, balloons ... Acceptable forms of payment include cash, cashier checks, and all major forms of credit cards.

Business Name: Cugini Florist   RENTON
                   413 S. 3rd St.
                   Renton, WA. 98057

Business Telephone Number: (425) 255-3900
                                  1(877) 284-4640
Business Website: www.cugini.com

Business Name: Malesis Flower   RENTON
                   313 Rainier Avenue So.
                   Renton, WA. 98057

Business Telephone Number: (425) 228-6622

Business Name: Alpine Nursery Incorporated   RENTON
                 16023 Se 144th St.
                 Renton, WA. 98059

Business Telephone Number: (425) 255-1598

Business Name: Seatac Flowers   SEATAC
                 19045 International Blvd.
                 Seatac, WA.98188

Business Telephone Number: (206) 244-9101
Business Website: www.seatacflowers.com

Business Name: Kent Floral   KENT
                 1401 Central Ave. S.
                 Kent, WA. 98032

Business Telephone Number: (253) 852-1970
                       1(800) 852-1977
Business Website: www.kentfloral.net

Business Name: Countryside Floral and Garden   ISSAQUAH
                 1420 NW Gilman Blvd. Ste. 1
                 Issaquah, WA. 98027

Business Telephone Number: (425) 392-0999
Business Website: countrysidefloral.com

Business Name: Squak Mt. Greenhouses and Nursery   ISSAQUAH
                 7600 Renton Issaquah Rd. Se.
                 Issaquah, WA. 98027

Business Telephone Number: (425) 392-1025
Business Website: www.squakmountainnursery.com

Business Name: Des Moines Florist   DES MOINES
721 S. 219th St.
Des Moines, WA. 98198

Business Telephone Number: (206) 824-5920

Business Name: Lake City Florist   LAKE CITY
11742 15th Ave. NE.
Lake City, WA. 98125

Business Telephone Number: (206) 364-4321

Business Name: The Flower Lady   SEATTLE
3230 Eastlake Avenue
Seattle, WA. 98102

Business Telephone Number: (206) 325-5751

Business Name: Topper's European Floral Design   SEATTLE
411 University Street
Seattle, WA. 98101

Business Telephone Number: (206) 622-6330

Business Name: Tomis Flower Shop   BURIEN
15607 1st Ave. S.
Burien, WA. 98148

Business Telephone Number: (206) 243-7670

Business Name: Gehl Flowers and Gifts   BURIEN
441 SW 152nd St.
Burien, WA. 98166

Business Telephone Number: (206) 242-3205

Business Name: Mercer Island Florist   MERCER ISLAND
               2728 78th Ave. Se.
               Mercer Island, WA. 98040

Business Telephone Number: (206)232-2990

Business Name: Edmonds Flower Shop   EDMONDS
               401 Main St.
               Edmonds, WA. 98020

Business Telephone Number: (425) 776-9105
                          1(888) 776-9119

Business Name: Carol's Maple Valley Floral   MAPLE VALLEY
               23220 Maple Valley Highway Se. Ste.11
               Maple Valley, WA. 98038

Business Telephone Number: (425) 432-1229
                          1(800) 531-9269
Business Website: www.carolsfloral.com

Business Name: Covington Floral Designs   COVINGTON
               15220 SE 272nd Street Ste. D
               Covington, WA. 98042

Business Telephone Number (253) 631-8046
Business Website: www.covingtonflorists.com

Business Name: TJ Blooms   BELLEVUE
               1313 156th Ave. NE, Ste. 225
               Bellevue, WA. 98007

Business Telephone Number: (425)643-4649
Business Website: www.tjblooms.com

FURNITURE REPAIR/REFINISHING/STRIPPING

Business Name: Jerry's Furniture Repair   KENT
                27516 132nd Ave. SE.
                Kent, WA. 98042

Business Telephone Number: (253) 630-9892

Business Name: Maple Valley Furniture Repair   MAPLE VALLEY
                1819 Central
                Kent, WA. 98032

Business Telephone Number: (253) 631-4003

GROCERIES

Business Name: Cedar River Market   RENTON
                     3418 Se. 6th St.
                     Renton, WA. 98058

Business Telephone Number: (425) 228-0758

Business Name: Cash and Carry   KENT
                     21504 84th Ave. S.
                     Kent, WA. 98032

Business Telephone Number: (253)872-7586

GYMNASTICS

Business Name: Gymnastics East   BELLEVUE
              13425 SE 30th St Ste. 2A
              Bellevue, WA. 98005

Business Telephone Number: (425) 644-8117
Business Website: www.gymnasticseast.com

Business Name: Elite Cheer Center   AUBURN
              1604 15th St. SW.
              Auburn, WA. 98001

Business Telephone Number: (253) 833-8030
Business Website: elitecheeranddance.com

Business Name: Auburn Gymnastics Center   AUBURN
              1601 Boundary Blvd.
              Auburn, WA. 98001

Business Telephone Number: (253) 876-9991
Business Website: www.auburngymnastics.com

Business Name: The Little Gym of Kent   KENT
              18437 E. Valley Highway
              Kent, WA. 98032

Business Telephone Number: (253) 656-0737
Business Website: www.tlgkentwa.com

Business Name: Gym Starz Gymnastics   KENT
            21440 68th Ave. S. Ste. 107
            Kent, WA. 98032

Business Telephone Number: (253) 639-9339
Business Website: www.gymstarzgym.com

Business Name: Metropolitan Gymnastics   KENT
            6822 S. 190th St.
            Kent, WA. 98032

Business Telephone Number: (206) 575-4138
Business Website: www.metropolitangym.com

Business Name: Gymagine Gymnastics   MUKILTEO
            3616 S. Rd. Ste. B3
            Mukilteo, WA. 98275

Business Telephone Number: (425) 513-8700
Business Website: www.gymagine.com

Business Name: Gymnastics Connection   WOODINVILLE
            14213 NE. 193rd Pl.
            Woodinville, WA. 98072

Business Telephone Number: (425) 486-6887
Business Website: www.gymnasticsconnection.com

Business Name: Northshore Gymnastics Center   WOODINVILLE
            19460 144th Ave. NE
            Woodinville. WA. 98072

Business Telephone Number: (425) 402-6602
Business Website: www.northshoregymnastics.com

Business Name: Max Gymnastics Academy   SEATAC
                19102 Des Moines Memorial Dr.
                Seatac, WA 98148

Business Telephone Number: (206) 439-8234

Business Name: Puget Sound School-Gymnastics   PUYALLUP
                1217 13th St. SE.
                Puyallup, WA. 98372

Business Telephone Number: (253) 845-0910

Business Name: Roach Gymnastics   SUMNER
                5914 Graham Ave.
                Sumner, WA. 98390

Business Telephone Number: (253) 826-5999

Business Name: Enumclaw Gymnastics Center   ENUMCLAW
                2251 Cole
                Enumclaw, WA. 98022

Business Telephone Number: (360) 802-9020
Business Website: www.enumclawgymnastics.com

Business Name: NASA Gymnastics   GIG HARBOR
                2509 Jahn Avenue NW #11
                Gig Harbor, WA. 98335

Business Telephone Number: (253) 851-7061
Business Website: www.nasagym.com

HEALTH: BEVERAGES/STORES/CLUBS

Business Name XanGo® Independent Distributors   KENT

Business Owner(s): Marv and Barb Kleven
Business Telephone Number: (253) 852-5944
                          (866) 469-0531
                          (425) 246-2326-cell
Business Website: www.mymangosteen.com/mbkleven

"XanGo® Juice boasts a proprietary whole–fruit formula, harnessing a con-
centrated rush of xanthones—a vigorous family of next–generation phyto-
nutrients. Research shows xanthones possess potent antioxidant properties
that may help maintain intestinal health, strengthen the immune system,
neutralize free radicals, help support cartilage and joint function, and promote a healthy seasonal respiratory system."

**These statements have not been evaluated by the FDA. This product is
not intended to diagnose, treat, cure or prevent any disease.

To learn more about XanGo® contact Marv and Barbara Kleven,
Independent XanGo® Distributors

Business Name: Nature's Way   KENT
                26011 104th Ave. Se.
                Kent, WA. 98030

Business Telephone Number: (253) 854-5395

Business Name: Kent Women's Aerobic and Fitness Center   KENT
                841 Central Ave. N.
                Kent, WA. 98032

Business Telephone Number: (253) 852-0747
Business Website: www.kentwomens.com

Business Name: Eagle Fitness Kent   KENT
                 23424 Pacific Highway S.
                 Kent, WA. 98032

Business Telephone Number: (253) 878-3788

Business Name: General Nutrition Center   KENT
                 26027 104th Ave. SE.
                 Kent, WA. 98032

Business Telephone Number: (253) 852-5071

Business Name: Marlene's Market and Deli   FEDERAL WAY
                 2565 So. Gateway Center Place
                 Federal Way, WA. 98003

Business Telephone Number: (253) 839-0933
Business Website: www.marlenesmarket-deli.com

Business Name: Minkler's Green Earth Nutrition   RENTON
                 125 Airport Way
                 Renton, WA. 98055

Business Telephone Number: (425) 226-7757

Business Name: Super Supplements   RENTON
                 707 Rainier Ave. S.
                 Renton, WA. 98057

Business Telephone Number: (425) 226-2112
Business Website: www.supersup.com

Business Name: Bally Total Fitness   RENTON
              17110 116th Ave. Se.
              Renton, WA. 98058

Business Telephone Number: (425) 271-3857

Business Name: Westcoast Fitness   RENTON
              1755 NE. 48th
              Renton, WA. 98056

Business Telephone Number: (425) 226-3808

Business Name: Enumclaw Wellness Center   ENUMCLAW
              856 Cole St.
              Enumclaw, WA. 98022

Business Telephone Number: (360) 825-7837

Business Name: Bonney Lake Fitness   BONNEY LAKE
              20800 State Rte. 410E
              Bonney Lake, WA. 98391

Business Telephone Number: (253) 863-4288

HOUSEWARES

Business Name: Tupperware®, Independent Director   MAPLE VALLEY
Business Owners(s): Saralyn Whitney
           PO Box 1406
           Maple Valley, WA. 98038

Business Telephone Number (206) 850-7946
Business Website: www.my.tupperware.com/saralyn

Tupperware is a well respected product line with a long history of inno-
vation and style. With their reliable line of kitchen ware, storage contain-
ers, serving dishes, gadgets and more … suitable products can be found
to meet the needs of all at an affordable price. If you would like to learn
about opportunities for custom kitchen consultations, fundraisers, parties,
and additional exciting products and great services from the #1 brand in
food storage, then this is your contact. Cash, check, Visa, MasterCard, and
Discover are acceptable forms of payment.

ICE CREAM

Business Name: Mix Ice Cream Bar   SEATTLE
                4507 University Way NE
                Seattle, WA. 98105

Business Telephone Number: (206) 547-3436

Business Name: Auntie Irene's Ice Cream Shoppe   DES MOINES
                22504 Marine View Dr. S.
                Des Moines, WA. 98198

Business Telephone Number: (206) 824-0249

Business Name: Marble Slab Creamery   MAPLE VALLEY
                23745 225th Way SE.
                Maple Valley, WA. 98038

Business Name: (425) 413-6701

ICE SKATING/ROLLER SKATING

Business Name: Tiffany's Skate Inn   PUYALLUP
                1113 Meridian Street North
                Puyallup, WA. 98371

Business Telephone Number: (253) 848-1153
Business Website: www.tiffanysskateinn.com

Business Name: Sprinker Recreation Center   SPANAWAY
                14824 C. St. S.
                Tacoma, WA. 98444

Business Telephone Number: (253) 798-4000

Business Name: Castle Ice   RENTON
                12620 164th Ave. SE.
                Renton, WA. 98059

Business Telephone Number: (425) 254-8750

JEWELRY

Business Name: Fun, Affordable, Fashionable Jewelry   RENTON
Business Owner: Aidé Gutierréz
Business Established in: 2006
Business Telephone Number: (425) 351-7412
Business email address: gabe-n-aide@comcast.net

Affordable, fun fashionable jewelry is now available for any occasion. Available through home shows and office shows, fundraisers, catalogue ... this fine line offers accessories fitting any budget. Call today to learn more about the latest stylish choices and wonderful career opportunities. Cash, cashiers checks, and all major credit credits are accepted except American Express.

Business Name: Jewels by Park Lane Inc©, Independent Distributor

                                                              RENTON
Business Owner(s): Lillie Hayden, Area Manager
Business Established in: Over 51 years in business

Business Telephone Number (425)255-7222
Business Website: www.myparklane.com/lhayden

Hours of Operation: Monday-Wednesday by appointment only
                    Thursday-Saturday 10:00am-6:00pm

Jewels by Park Lane© features magnificent, fashionable jewelry that is luxurious and elegant while offering distinction with each style. During their 50 plus year history, Jewels by Park Lane© has become your one stop shop jewelry representative with its line of Casual jewelry, Classic jewelry, After Five jewelry, Sportswear jewelry and Career-Wear jewelry. Take a look today, to see what you have been missing. Cash, cashiers checks, and major credit cards are accepted.

Business Name: KP Limited   COVINGTON
Business Owner: Karen Patterson
Business Established in: 2005
Business Address: 26422 189th Ave. SE.
                  Covington, WA. 98042

Business Telephone Number: (253) 740-3150
Business Website: www.kplimited.com

KP Limited offers a variety of products to satisfy anyones fashion sense. Specializing in custom jewelry, clothing, and embroidery this is the business that "never closes" and works with you to help meet your fashion needs. Cash, cashiers checks, money orders, MasterCard, Visa, American Express, Discover and PayPal are all acceptable forms of payment.

Business Name: D'Original Jewelers   BELLEVUE
                885 Bellevue Way NE
                Bellevue, WA. 98004

Business Telephone Number: (253) 454-5559

Business Name: Allan Turner Jewelers   EDMONDS
                408 Main St.
                Edmonds, WA. 98020

Business Telephone Number: (425) 546-1211
Business Website: www.allanturnerjewelers.com

LANDSCAPING

Business Name: Vo's Landscaping and Gardening   KENT
Business Telephone Number: (253) 632-1244

Business Name: Bac's Landscaping   KENT
Business Telephone Number: (253) 630-6258

MAGICIAN

Business Name: C Allan The Silk Master   RENTON
Business Telephone Number: (425) 235-4845

MARTIAL ARTS/FITNESS TRAINING

Business Name: Dragon Center Family Karate   FEDERAL WAY
35417 21st Ave. SW.
Federal Way, WA. 98023

Business Telephone Number: (253) 952- 3656

Business Name: West Seattle Aikikai   WEST SEATTLE
4101 West Marginal Way
Seattle, WA. 98106

Business Telephone Number: (206) 935-3598

Business Name: Giant Tae Kwon Do   RENTON
17056 116th Ave. Se.
Renton, WA. 98058

Business Telephone Number: (425) 235-0298

Business Name: Fairwood Martial Arts   RENTON
14133 SE 171st Way
Renton, WA. 98058

Business Telephone Number: (425) 255-8144
Business Website: fairwoodmartialarts.com

Business Name: Lee's Martial Arts   RENTON
405 S. 3rd St
Renton, WA. 98055

Business Telephone Number: (425) 255-4549
Business Website: www.leesmartialarts.org

Business Name: Kim's Tae Kwon Do   RENTON
               4602 NE. Sunset Blvd.
               Renton, WA. 98059

Business Telephone Number: (425) 254-3526
Business Website: www.kimstkd-renton.com

Business Name: Covington School of Karate   COVINGTON
               27019 35th S.
               Covington, WA. 98032

Business Telephone Number: (253) 639-0697

Business Name: Emerald City Tae Kwon Do   COVINGTON
               18527 SE. 272nd St.
               Covington, WA. 98042

Business Telephone Number: (253) 630-4450
Business Website: www.emeraldcitytkd.com

Business Name: Karate Northwest   AUBURN
               2818 Auburn Way N.
               Auburn, WA. 98002

Business Telephone Number: (253) 833-7317

Business Name: AMC Kickboxing and Pankration   KIRKLAND
               427 6th St. S.
               Kirkland, WA. 98033

Business Telephone Number (425) 822-9656
Business Website: www.pankration.com

Business Name: Aikido School of Self Defense   REDMOND
8460 164th Ave. NE.
Redmond, WA. 98052

Business Telephone Number: (425) 558-2996
Business Website: www. northwestnga.com

Business Name: Greenlake Martial Arts School   SEATTLE
319 NE. 72nd St.
Seattle, WA. 98115

Business Telephone Number: (206) 522-2457
Business Website: www. newkungfu.com

Business Name: Shins Tae Kwon Do Academy   KENMORE
6524 NE. 181st. St.
Kenmore, WA. 98028

Business Telephone Number: (206) 402-8900

Business Name: Elite Martial Arts and Family Success Center KENMORE
6810 NE. 153rd. Pl
Kenmore, WA. 98028

Business Telephone Number: (206) 820-5425

Business Name: Shaolin Kung Fu Academy   PUYALLUP
10109 122nd St. SE.
Puyallup, WA. 98373

Business Telephone Number: (253) 848-2160

Business Name: Premier Martial Arts Academy   PUYALLUP
12623 Meridian E.
Puyallup, WA. 98373

Business Telephone Number: (253) 848-5425

Business Name: Bennest Karate School   EDGEWOOD
2908 Meridian Ave.E.
Edgewood, WA. 98371

Business Telephone Number: (253) 864-7131

Business Name: Lions Way Martial Arts   KENT
10603 Se. 240th St.
Kent, WA. 98031

Business Telephone Number: (253) 856-2122

Business Name: United Studios of Self Defense   KENT
20619 108th Ave. SE.
Kent, WA. 98031

Business Telephone Number: (253) 854-5056

Business Name: Seattle Tae Kwon Do Academy   NORMADY PARK
801 SW. 174th St.
Seattle, WA. 98166

Business Telephone Number: (206) 444-9473

MURALS

Business Name: Donna Hennig Mural Design   RENTON
Business Telephone Number: (425) 228-5971
Business Website: www.muraldesign.com

NEEDLEWORK/MATERIALS

Business Name: Knittery   RENTON
                601 S. Grady Way
                Renton, WA. 98055

Business Telephone Number: (425) 228-4694

PAINTING

Business Name: Delucia's Professional Painting Company   RENTON
Business Owner(s): Victor DeLucia
Business Established In: 1990
Business Telephone Number: (425) 235-0457 (office)
Business Website: www.deluciaspainting.com

Delucia's painting is the place to contact for all your interior and exterior painting needs. Praised for their attention to detail, this company specializes in "occupied homes."
Their offerings include: high quality/affordable prices, licensed/bonded/insured, custom colors, walls-ceilings-woodwork, acoustical ceilings, White Glove cleanup, many local references, free estimates. To meet your needs give Vic a call today.

Business Name: Horizon Painting Services   RENTON
5351 NE. 2nd St. Bldg. B
Renton, WA. 98059

Business Telephone Number: (425) 235-8680

Business Name: Long Painting Company   KENT
21414 68th Ave. S.
Kent, WA. 98032

Business Telephone Number: (253) 234-8050
Business Website: www.longpainting.com

PARTIES-SUPPLIES/RENTALS/SALES

Business Name: Astro Jump   TUKWILA
            930 Industry Drive
            Tukwila, WA. 98188

Business Telephone Number: (206) 575-1434
                        1-800-244-5867
Business Website: www.astrojump.com

Business Name: Merry Makers   TACOMA
            1401 B-South Sprague Ave.
            Tacoma, WA. 98405

Business Telephone Number: (253) 572-0172
                        1(800) 585-1500
Business Website: www.merrymakers.net

Business Name: American Party Place   TACOMA
            4522 S. Tacoma Way
            Tacoma, WA. 98409

Business Telephone Number: (253) 473-3300
Business Website: www.americanpartyplace.com

Business Name: Party Etc.   MAPLE VALLEY
            27317 Maple Valley-Black Diamond Rd.
            Maple Valley, WA. 98038

Business Telephone Number: (425) 433-0119

Business Name: Abbey Party Rents   SEATTLE
               1310 N. 131st
               Seattle, WA. 98133

Business Telephone Number: (206) 362-3222
Business Website: abbeypartyrents.com

PET GROOMING

Business Name: Tender Care Mobile Grooming Service   BELLEVUE
Business Owner(s): Debbie Pearson, JoAnn Russell

Business Telephone Number: (253) 941-9663

POTTERY

Business Name: Patsy's Pottery   REDMOND
                P.O. Box 2311
                Redmond, WA. 98073

Business Telephone Number: (425) 868-3989
Business Website: www.patsyspottery.com

Business Name: Bonsai Northwest   TUKWILA
                5021 S. 144th St.
                Tukwila, WA. 98168

Business Telephone Number: (206) 242-8244
Business Website: www.bonsainw.com

Business Name: Half Price Pots   RENTON
                208 SW. 16th St.
                Renton, WA. 98057

Business Telephone Number: (425) 687-9200
Business Website: www.halfpricepots.com

PRINTERS

Business Name: Just Your Type Printing
Owner(s): Stephanie Fife
Business Established in: 1996
Business Telephone Number: (206) 390-8414
Business Website: www.JustYourTypePrinting.com
Business Address: PO Box 2146
               Renton, WA. 98056

Hours of Operation: Monday-Thursday ... by appointment, Web & Email 24/7

Located in Renton, Washington this dynamic printer has become a leading contender in offering high quality graphic design and print services with superior customer service. With a vast number of years in business and continual recognition for their flexibility Just Your Type Printing has the ability to meet the needs of consumers no matter how large or small the job. Acceptable forms of payment: cash, check.

Business Name: Alphagraphics Print Shop of the Future   RENTON
                433 SW. 41st St.
                Renton, WA. 98057

Business Telephone Number: (425) 251-9888

Business Name: Renton Printery   RENTON
                315 S. 3rd St.
                Renton, WA. 98057

Business Telephone Number: (425) 235-1776

PRODUCE

Business Name: Greenfresh Market   RENTON
575 Rainier Avenue North
Renton, WA. 98057

Business Name: Lenny's Market   RENTON
757 Rainier S.
Renton, WA. 98055

Business Telephone Number: (425) 271-5910

Business Name: Valley Harvest   KENT
23636 104th Ave. SE.
Kent, WA. 98031

Business Telephone Number: (253) 856-8462

Business Name: Uwajimaya Incorporated   SEATTLE
600 5th Ave. S.
Seattle, WA. 98104

Business Telephone Number: (206) 624-6248

Business Name: Rising Sun Farm and Produce   SEATTLE
6505 15th Ave. NE.
Seattle, WA. 98115

Business Telephone Number: (206) 524-9741

Business Name: Tacoma Boys   PUYALLUP
903 39th Ave. SW.
Puyallup, WA. 98373

Business Telephone Number: (253) 864-8568

RESTAURANT/FOOD SERVICES

Business Name: Armondo's Café Italiano   RENTON
Business Owners(s) Armondo and Angela Pavone
Business Established in: 1986
Business Telephone Number: (425) 228-0759
Business Website: www.armondos.com
Business Address: 310 Wells Avenue South
                  Renton, WA. 98057

Hours of Operation: Monday-Thursday 11:00am-9:00pm
                    Friday 11:00am-10pm
                    Saturday 4:00pm-10:00pm
                    Sunday 4:00pm-9:00pm

Armondo's Café Italiano, a Renton family tradition for over twenty years, features a large, full-service bar, hand-blown glass lighting fixtures, cozy seats around the wood fired pizza oven, and plenty of family-friendly seating at booths and tables. There is a private dining room suitable for business meetings and parties of up to 16 guests. The main dining room can accommodate parties of up to 40 guests. Armondo's is recognized for their wood-fired pizza and calzones, Italian classics, Osso Bucco, and signature dish "Chicken Armondo."

Business Name: Melrose Grill   RENTON
Business Owners: Kimberly Searing, Armondo Pavone
Business Established in: 2002
Business Telephone Number: (425) 254-0759
Business Website: www.melrosegrill.com
Business Address: 819 Houser Way S.
                  Renton, WA. 98057

Hours of Operation: Open at 5:00pm daily

A great neighborhood steakhouse serving dry—aged Mid-west steak with a supporting cast of seafood, pork and chicken, fine wines and specialty drinks to accompany your meal. Acceptable payments: cash, Visa, Mastercard, American Express, checks

Business Name: Whistle Stop Ale House   RENTON
Business Established in: 1995
Business Telephone Number: (425) 277-3039
Business Website: www.whistlestopalehouse.com
Business Address: 809 S. 4th Street
                 Renton, WA. 98055

Hours of Operation: Monday-Thursday 11:00am-10:00pm, Friday 11:00am-12:00am, Saturday 9:00am-12:00am, Sunday 9:00am-9:00pm, closed most holidays

Business Name: Momma's Teriyaki and Pho   RENTON
Business Telephone Number: (425) 227-8482
Business Address: 16928 116th Ave Se.
                 Renton, WA. 98058

Hours of Operation: Monday-Friday 11:00am-8:00pm
                    Saturday 12:00pm-8:00pm

Business Name: Pabla Indian Cuisine   RENTON
Business Established in: 1947, in Renton since 1998
Business Telephone Number: (425) 228-4625
Business Website: www.pablacuisine.com
Business Address: 364 Renton Center Way SW, #C-60
                 Renton, WA. 98055

Hours of Operation: Restaurant 11:00am-3:00pm (buffet)
                    5:00pm-10:00pm (dinner)
                    Grocery Hours: 11:00am-10:00pm

Business Name: Pho' Hoa Noodle Soup   RENTON
Business Owner: John Lu
Business Telephone Number: (425) 204-9991
Business Website: www.phohoa.com
Business Address: 801 S. 3rd St.
               Renton, WA. 98055

Hours of Operation: Monday-Sunday 9:00am-9:00pm

Business Name: Plum Delicious Family Restaurant   RENTON
Business Telephone Number: (425) 255-8510
Business Address: 3212 NE Sunset Blvd.
               Renton, WA. 98056

Hours of Operation: Monday-Thursday 7:00am-9:00pm
                     Friday-Sunday 7:00am-10:00pm

Business Name: Pounders Bar and Grill   RENTON
Business Owner: Andrew Boe
Business Telephone Number: (425) 254-3800
Business Address: 221 Main Avenue South
               Renton, WA. 98055

Hours of Operation: Monday-Sunday 11:30am -2:00am

Business Name: Royal Orchid Thai Restaurant   RENTON
Business Owner: Kane Bunyaketu
Business Telephone Number: (425) 271-4219
Business Address: 104 Rainier Avenue So.
               Renton, WA. 98055

Hours of Operation: Monday-Thursday 11:00am-9:30pm
                     Friday-Saturday 11:00am-10:00pm
                     Sunday 11:00am-9:30pm

Business Name: T.L. Café and Bar   RENTON
Business Owner: Sean Nguyen
Business Telephone Number (425) 271-8240
Business Address: 340 Burnett Avenue
            Renton, WA. 98055

Hours of Operation: Monday-Sunday 2:00pm-2:00

Business Name: The Met Coffee and Wine Bar   RENTON
            232-C Burnett Ave. S
            Renton, WA. 98055
Business Owner: Michael Servis
Business Telephone Number: (425) 687-7989
Business Website: www.themetwinebar.com

Hours of Operation: Monday-Thursday 7:00am-9:00pm
            Friday 7:00am-10:00pm
            Saturday 8:00am-10:00pm
            Sunday 12:00pm-6:00pm

Business Name: The Yankee Grill   RENTON
Business Address: One S. Grady Way
            Renton, WA. 98055
General Manager: John Engel

Business Telephone Number: (425)255-8543

Hours of Operation: Monday-Saturday 6:00am-11pm
            Sunday 6:00am-10:00pm

Business Name: DC's Bar and Grill   RENTON
Business Owners(s): Casey Reinke, Daniela Lapizco
Business Address: 907 S. 3rd St.
            Renton, WA. 98057

Business Telephone Number: (425) 255-2511

Hours of Operation: Monday-Sunday 11:00am-10:00pm

Business Name: Belle Napoli Ristorante Italiano   RENTON
Business Owner: Ciro D'onofrio
Business Address: 509-A South 3rd Street
                 Renton. WA. 98055

Business Telephone Number: (425) 277-8200

Hours of Operation: Lunch Tuesday-Friday 11:00am-2:00pm
                    Dinner Tuesday-Friday 5:00pm-close

Business Name: Vino's Ristorante Italiano   RENTON
Business Address: 212 S. Third St.
                 Renton, WA. 98055
Business Telephone Number: (425) 271-7042
Business Website: www.ristorantevino.com

Hours of Operation: Lunch Monday-Friday 11:00am-2:00pm
                    Dinner Monday-Sunday 5:00pm-10:00pm

Business Name: Bill's Bodacious BBQ   RENTON
Business Owners: Bill McGraw, Carol McGraw
Business Address: 3813 NE 4th
                 Renton, WA. 98056

Business Telephone Number: (425) 255-0535

Hours of Operation: Tuesday-Saturday 11:00am-9:00pm
                    Sunday 12:30pm-8:00pm

Business Name: 3 Sisters BBQ   RENTON
Business Address: 509-B S. 3rd St.
            Renton, WA. 98056

Business Telephone Number: (425) 277-5076

Business Name: Cedar River Smokehouse   RENTON
Business Address: 304 Wells Ave. S.
            Renton, WA. 98058

Business Telephone Number: (425) 255-4820
Business Website: www.crshbbq.com

Hours of Operation: Monday-Saturday 11:00am-8:00pm
            Sunday 12:00pm-8:00pm

Business Name: Stiffy's Bar and Grill   RENTON
            919 3rd Ave. S.
            Renton, WA. 98055

Business Telephone Number: (425) 282-5395

Business Name: General's BBQ   KENT
Business Address: 19249 84th Ave. S.
            Kent, WA. 98032

Business Telephone Number: (253) 437-5250
Business Website: www.thegeneralsbbq.com

Hours of Operation: Monday-Friday 10:00am-6:00pm
            Saturday 12:00pm-6:00pm
            Sunday 12:00-6:00pm

Business Name: Bittersweet   KENT
Business Address: 211 First Avenue So.
              Kent, WA. 98032

Business Telephone Number: (253) 854-0707
Business Website: www.bittersweetofkent.com

Hours of Operation: Monday-Saturday 10:00am-4:00pm
              Friday 10:00am-8:00pm

Business Name: Andy's Restaurant and Lounge   KENT
Business Address: 623 Central Avenue
              Kent, WA. 98032

Business Telephone Number (253) 859-4800

Hours of Operation: Monday-Friday 6:00am-6:00pm
              Saturday-Sunday 8:00am-4:00pm
              Lounge open until 2:00am/features full menu

Business Name: Wingdome   KENT
              21008 108th SE
              Kent, WA. 98031

Business Telephone Number: (253) 854-9464
Hours of Operation: Monday 11:30am-10:00pm
              Tuesday/Wednesday/Thursday 11:30am-10:00pm
              Friday/Saturday 11:30am-11:00pm
              Sunday 11:30am-9:00pm

Business Name: Chuck's Daily Special   KENT
              19625 62nd Ave. S, B-102
              Kent, WA. 98032

Business Telephone Number: (253) 395-1515
Business Website: www.chucksdailyspecial.com

Hours of Operation: Monday-Friday 7:00am-3:00pm

Business Name: Angelo's of Burien   BURIEN
Business Address: 601 SW 153rd
        Burien, WA.

Business Telephone Number: (206) 244-3555
Business Website: www.angelosofburien.com

Hours of Operation: Monday-Saturday 11:00am-2:00pm
        Sunday 5:00pm-9:00pm

Business Name: Athens Pizza and Spaghetti House   AUBURN
        959 E. Main Street
        Auburn, WA. 98002

Business Telephone Number: (253) 939-7444

Hours of Operation: Monday-Thursday 11:00am-10:00pm
        Friday 11:00am-11:00 pm
        Saturday 4:00pm-10:00pm
        Sunday 4:00 pm-10:00pm

Business Name: C Street Café and Teriyaki   AUBURN
        3411 C. Street NE.
        Auburn, WA. 98002

Business Telephone Number: (253) 939-7270

Hours of Operation: Monday-Friday 7:00am-3:00pm

Business Name: The Oak Tree Café   AUBURN
                2801 C St. SW.
                Auburn, WA. 98001

Business Telephone Number: (253) 735-8560

Hours of Operation: Monday-Friday 7:00am-2:00pm

Business Name: Performance Grill   AUBURN
                1525 A St. NE.
                Auburn, WA.

Business Telephone Number: (253) 804-5506
Business Website: www.performancegrill.com

Hours of Operation: Restaurant Monday-Sunday 7:00am-10:00pm
                    Lounge Monday-Sunday 7:00am-2:00am

Business Name: The Pit Restaurant and Bar   AUBURN
                102 W. Main
                Auburn, WA. 98001

Business Telephone Number: (253) 735-7101

Business Name: Rio Blanco Family Mexican Restaurant   AUBURN
                3830 A. Street SE.
                Auburn, WA. 98002

Business Telephone Number: (253) 939-9311

Hours of Operation: Monday-Thursday 10:30am-10:00pm
                    Friday/Saturday 10:30am-11:00pm
                    Sunday 10:30am-10:00pm

Business Name: Big Daddy's Drive Inn   AUBURN
                1138 Auburn Way
                Auburn, WA. 98002

Business Telephone Number: (253) 833-7255

Hours of Operation: Monday-Thursday 10:30am-8:30pm
                    Friday/Saturday 10:30-9:00pm
                    Sunday 10:30am-8:00pm

Business Name: Charlestown Street Café   WEST SEATTLE
                3800 California Ave. SW.
                Seattle, WA. 98116

Business Telephone Number: (206) 937-3800

Hours of Operation: Monday-Sunday 6:00am-9:00pm

Business Name: Jak's Grill   WEST SEATTLE
                4548 California Ave. SW.
                Seattle, WA. 98116

Business Telephone Number: (206) 937-7809

Hours of Operation: Lunch Tuesday-Friday 11:00am-2:00pm
                    Dinner Monday 5:00pm-9:00pm
                    Tuesday-Thursday 5:00pm-10:00pm
                    Friday 4:30pm-11:00pm
                    Saturday 4:00-11:00pm
                    Sunday 4:00pm-9:00pm

Business Name: Pegasus Pizza   WEST SEATTLE
                2758 Alki Avenue SW.
                Seattle, WA. 98116

Business Telephone Number: (206) 932-4849

Hours of Operation: Monday-Friday 11:30am-11:00pm
Saturday 12:00pm-11:00pm
Sunday 12:00pm-11:00pm

Business Name: Buzzy's Greenwater Café　　　　ENUMCLAW
58423 State Route 410 E.
Enumclaw, WA. 98022

Business Telephone Number: (360) 663-2421

Hours of Operation: Monday-Closed
Tuesday-Friday 6:00am-2:00pm
Saturday/Sunday 6:00am-3:00pm

Business Name: Café Panini　　　　ENUMCLAW
1537 Cole Street
Enumclaw, WA. 98022

Business Telephone Number: (360) 802-5132
Business Website: www.cafepanini.net

Hours of Operation: Monday-Saturday Lunch 10:30am-3:00pm
Monday-Friday　Dinner 4:00pm-9:00pm
Saturday Dinner　4:00pm-10:00pm
Sunday-Closed

Business Name: Coho's Winebar and Seafood Grill　　　　BUCKLEY
737 Main Street
Buckley, WA. 98321

Business Telephone Number: (360) 829-5082

Hours of Operation: Tuesday-Thursday 4:00pm-9:00pm
Friday/Saturday 4:30pm-9:30pm
Sunday 4:00pm-9:00pm

Business Name: Mezcal Mexican Restaurant   BUCKLEY
818 Main Street
Buckley, WA. 98321

Business Telephone Number: (360) 829-5276

Hours of Operation: Monday-Sunday 11:00am-9:00pm

Business Name: New China Buffet   PUYALLUP
4215 S. Meridian
Puyallup, WA. 98373

Business Telephone Number: (253) 770-3888

Hours of Operation: Monday-Thursday 11:00am-10:00pm
Friday/Saturday 11:00am-11:00pm
Sunday 11:00am-10:00pm

Business Name: Hangar Inn   PUYALLUP
16919A Meridian East
Puyallup, WA. 98373

Business Telephone Number: (253) 848-7516

Hours of Operation: Monday–Thursday 6:00am-9:00pm
Friday/Saturday 6:00am-10:00pm
Sunday 6:00am-9:00pm

Business Name: Cattin's Family Dining   PUYALLUP
105 9th Avenue SW
Puyallup, WA. 98371

Business Telephone Number: (253) 848-3494

Hours of Operation: Open 24 Hours per Day

Business Name: Burger Han's   FEDERAL WAY
212 SW. 336th
Federal Way, WA. 98023

Business Telephone Number: (253) 661-6697

Hours of Operation: Monday-Saturday 11:00am-9:00pm
Sunday-closed

Business Name: Gino's Bistro   FEDERAL WAY
4624 SW. 320th
Federal Way. WA. 98023

Business Telephone Number: (253) 815-1215

Hours of Operation: Monday-Thursday 11:30am-9:30pm
Friday 11:00am-10:00pm
Saturday 1:00pm-10:00pm
Sunday 1:00pm-9:30pm

Business Name: Akasaka Restaurant   FEDERAL WAY
31407-H Pacific Highway S
Federal Way, WA.

Business Telephone Number: (253) 946-3858
Business Website: www.akasakaseattle.com

Hours of Operation: Monday-Saturday 11:00am-10:00pm
Sunday 3:00pm-10:00pm

Business Name: Paul's Burger/Teriyaki   FEDERAL WAY
2148 South 314th Street
Federal Way, WA. 98003

Business Telephone Number: (253) 941-2618

Hours of Operation: Monday-Saturday 10:30am-8:30pm
Sunday 12:00pm-7:00pm

Business Name: Verrazano's   FEDERAL WAY
28835 Pacific Hwy S.
Federal Way, WA. 98003

Business Telephone Number: (253) 946-4122

Hours of Operation: Monday-Thursday 11:00am-10:00pm
Friday–Saturday 11:00am-11:00pm
Sunday 11:00am-10:00pm

Business Name: The Herbfarm   WOODINVILLE
14590 NE 145th Street
Woodinville, WA. 98072

Business Telephone Number: (425) 485-5300
Business Website: www.theherbfarm.com

Hours of Operation: Call for seating information (9 course meal)

Business Name: Racha Thai Restaurant   WOODINVILLE
13317 NE 175th Street
Woodinville, WA. 98072

Business Telephone Number: (425) 481-8833

Hours of Operation: Monday-Thursday 11:00am-9:00pm
Friday/Saturday 11:00am-10:00pm
Sunday 12:00pm-9:00pm
Closed Monday-Friday 3:00pm-4:00pm

Business Name: Warthog Barbeque Pit   FIFE
4921 20th Street East
Fife, Washington 98424

Business Telephone Number: (253) 896-5091
Business Website: http://www.warthogbbq.com/review.htm

Hours of Operation: Monday-Thursday 11:00am-8:00pm
Friday/Saturday 11:00am-9:00pm
Sunday 12:00pm-8:00pm

Business Name: Ristorante Isabella   COVINGTON
27116 167th Pl. SE.
Covington, WA. 98042

Business Telephone Number: (253) 630-3450

Hours of Operation: Lunch Tuesday-Friday 11:30am-2:00pm
Dinner Monday-Saturday 5:00pm-9:00pm

Business Name: Benjarong Thai Cuisine   COVINGTON
17017 SE 270th Pl, Suite 102
Covington, WA. 98042

Business Telephone Number: (253) 638-0085

Hours of Operation: Monday-Thursday 11:00am-9:00pm
Friday/Saturday 11:00am-10:00pm
Sunday 12:00pm-9:00pm

Business Name: Black Diamond Bakery and Restaurant
32805 Railroad Avenue   BLACK DIAMOND
Black Diamond, WA. 98010

Business Telephone Number: (360) 886-2235
Business Website: www.blackdiamondbakery.com

Hours of Operation: Monday-Friday 7:00am-3:00pm
Saturday/Sunday 7:00am-4:00pm

Business Name: La Louisiana Restaurant   SEATTLE
                2514 East Cherry
                Seattle, WA. 98122

Business Telephone Number (206) 329-5007

Business Name: Philadelphia Fevre Steak and Hoagie Shop   SEATTLE
                2332 East Madison Street
                Seattle, WA. 98112

Business Telephone Number: (206) 323-1000
Business Website: www.phillysteakshop.com

SWIMMING

Business Name: Atlantis Aquatics   RENTON
Business Owner(s): Mary Asman
Business Established in: 2000
Business Telephone Number: (425) 255-4339
Business Website: www.atlantis-aquatics.com

For the past eight years swimming has defined Mary's life. She started working for King County Pools in 1997 and started Atlantis Aquatics in 2000. The American Red Cross has certified her as both a Water Safety Instructor and Life Guard. In addition, she is trained in CPR. Continuing training ensures these certifications are current. To learn more about classes available at this facility give her a call.

Business Name: Swimmer's Lane   RENTON
Business Owner(s): Jerry and Jennifer Blanchard
Business Telephone Number: (425) 413-7946
Business Website: www.swimmerslane.com

TATTOOING

Business Name: Action Tattoo   AUBURN
               416 East Main St.
               Auburn, WA. 98002

Business Telephone Number: (253) 218-0358

Business Name: Ancient Arts Tattoo   RENTON
               928 S. Third St.
               Renton, WA. 98057

Business Telephone Number: (425) 938-2828
                           1(866) We Tat2U
Business Website: www.aatattoo.com

Business Name: Diamond Tattoo/Body Piercing   RENTON
               1017 Bronson Way S.
               Renton, WA. 98055

Business Telephone Number: (425) 227-8282
Business Website: www.diamondtattooandbodypiercing.com

Business Name: Ground Zero Tattoo and Body Piercing   BUCKLEY
               754 Main St.
               Buckley, WA. 98321

Business Telephone Number: (360) 829-1668

Business Name: House of Tattoo   TACOMA
                2701 6th Ave.
                Tacoma, WA. 98406

Business Telephone Number: (253)-274-8282

Business Name: Seven Deuce Tattoos and Body Piercing   FEDERAL WAY
                29500 Pacific Highway So.
                Federal Way, WA. 98003

Business Telephone Number: (253) 529-0881

Business Name: Fenix Tattoo   SEATTLE
                106 1st Ave. S.
                Seattle, WA. 98104

Business Telephone Number: (206) 623-1090

Business Name: Seattle Tattoo Emporium   SEATTLE
                1106 Pike St.
                Seattle, WA. 98101

Business Telephone Number: (206) 622-6895
Business Website: www.tattooemporiums.com

Business Name: Laughing Buddah Tattoo   SEATTLE
                219 Broadway E. Ste. 24
                Seattle, WA. 98102

Business Telephone Number: (206) 329-8274
Business Website: www.laughingbuddahtattoo.com

Business Name: Kent Dermagraphics   KENT
                118 Central Ave. N.
                Kent, WA. 98032

Business Telephone Number: (253) 852-2550

Business Name: A Sin on Skin   BURIEN
                421 ½ SW 152nd
                Burien, WA. 98166

Business Telephone Number: (206) 439-1636

THRIFT SHOPS

Business Name: More Pennies From Heavan   ENUMCLAW
                1749 Cole
                Enumclaw, WA. 98022

Business Telephone Number: (360) 802-9945

Business Name: St. Vincent De Paul   RENTON
                2825 Sunset Blvd NE.
                Renton, WA. 98056

Business Telephone Number: (425) 226-9426

Business Name: Value Village   RENTON
                1222 Bronson Way N.
                Renton, WA. 98057

Business Telephone Number: (425) 255-5637

TRANSPORTATION

Business Name: NA Charters   KENT
                         8721 S. 218th St.
                         Kent, WA. 98031

Business Telephone Number: (253) 872-7789
                                (866) 840-0757

WINDOW REPLACEMENT

Business Name: Emerald City Energy Inc.   RENTON
Business Telephone Number: (425) 228-1792
Business Website: www.emeraldcityenergy.com

WOMEN ORGANIZATIONS

Business Name: Women's Showcase   RENTON
Business Established in: 2005
Business Telephone Number: (425) 277-2950
Business Website: www.swanneerivers.com

Women who own their own businesses unite monthly to form a network of business opportunities. Information is available about each business; products are displayed and available for purchase, as well as an array of information is made available for those interested in venturing out on their own. This "mini bazaar" allows women to showcase their talents and reach their full potential in a safe environment. The showcases are held monthly at the Renton Community Center, 1715 Maple Valley Highway, Renton, WA. Children are always welcome and this free event is open to the public. If you have ever thought about spreading your wings and displaying your hidden talent, this is the time.

YARN SHOPS

Business Name: Knittery   RENTON
                601 S. Grady Way
                Renton, WA. 98055

Business Telephone Number: (425) 228-4694

Business Name: Nancy's Knits   RENTON
                17174 116th SE.
                Renton, WA. 98058

Business Telephone Number: (425) 255-7392

Business Name: The Yarn Stash   BURIEN
                615 SW. 152nd
                Burien, WA. 98166

Business Telephone Number: (206) 246-2727
Business Website: www.burienyarnstash.com

Business Name: Hilltop Yarn   SEATTLE
                2224 Queen Anne Avenue N.
                Seattle, WA. 98109

Business Telephone Number: (206) 282-1332
Business Website: www.hilltopyarn.com

Business Name: Full Circle   SEATTLE
                2036 NW. 56th St.
                Seattle. WA. 98107

Business Telephone Number: (206) 783-3322
Business Website: www.fullcircle.seattle.citysearch.com

Business Name: Acorn Street Shop   SEATTLE
                2818 NE.55th St.
                Seattle, WA. 98105

Business Telephone Number: (206) 525-1726
                           (800) 987-6354
Business Website: www.acornstreet.com

Business Name: NW Handspun Yarns   BELLINGHAM
                1401 Commercial St.
                Bellingham, WA. 98225

Business Telephone Number: (360) 783-0167
Business Website: www.nwhandspunyarns.com

Business Name: Friend's Knitting   VASHON ISLAND
                17205 Vashon Highway, Ste. D-4
                Vashon, WA. 98074

Business Telephone Number: (206) 819-3186
Business Website: www.friendsknitting.com

TESTIMONIALS ABOUT SUPPORTING SMALL BUSINESSES

"I really appreciate the quality of workmanship you get from small businesses. The owners and employees are invested in me. That's right! They make sure the goods and services I need are always of top quality. They treat me as if I am a part of their family. In fact, I know all of the small business owners I do business with on a first name basis. They are my friends. As such, they go the extra mile always to see I get my goods and services on time. If they make a mistake they make it right as quickly and painlessly as possible. Even when I make a mistake, they go above and beyond to make sure my mistake does not become a detriment of any kind. When I walk through the door of a small business, I know that my needs are their priority."

Former Police Officer, Steven P. Brown, Denver, CO.

"I really like to deal with small businesses because you get more of a personal interaction, plus you help to support the local economy. The Soggy Doggy Dog Wash is one such business that I really like to work with, as is Marine View Veterinary Clinic-both very personable. They remember you when you come in-you're not just a number."

Small Business Owner, Elynn Clayton, Dallas and Pals, Kent, WA.

"I truly appreciate the small business owner because of the quality they bring to various areas. The service you receive from small businesses is far better because owners have time to deal with their customers and the patience as well. You can tell small businesses are not solely concerned with just making a sale."

Small Business Owner, Barbara Winfrey, Bismarck, AR.

"There are plenty of places these days where people can search & buy products & services...personally even if I wasn't a small business owner...I have always preferred to do business with local small businesses. One of the big bonuses is you usually get terrific service & a chance to meet new people & support people in your own community. In my experience as a small business owner, I'd say at least 95% of my clients have turned into great friendships as well & not just a sale...which in turn makes your job not something you **have** to do every day...but a fun thing you **get** to do every day!"

Small Business Owner, Stephanie Dejong-Fife, <u>Just Your Type Printing</u>, Renton, WA.

"I support small businesses because I enjoy the people and employees found within them. You can usually find quality products and prices. I have been so impressed with the customer service found within most that I plan to start my own small business one day."

Future Small Business Owner. Willie Turner

TIPS FOR RUNNING A SUCCESSFUL SMALL BUSINESS

Be true to your word. If you tell a client you will take care of a particular task then by all means do it. Say what you mean and mean what you say.

Be prompt-there is nothing worse than to be kept waiting. If you are expected at a particular time arrive on time or better yet early. This makes a lasting impression.

Be organized and prepared. Have your business prepped and ready to function at a moments notice. When a client sees you are confident, they will have confidence in you as well.

Show respect at all times, even when your patience is tested. A soothing heart and tone can calm the most hyper nerves.

Always be prepared and have a plan. If your first ideas fail, knowing Plan B is ready is an added assurance.

Have a budget and spend within your means. There may be occasions when payments come in late, and preparing for that rainy day might just be the one thing that keeps your business from sinking.

Networking is a valuable resource. You can always learn from others in the field. Never be too proud to learn from someone else. Ask questions when needed or uncertain. Share your dreams and discuss common goals.

Stay in the game. Businesses are constantly changing and new products are continually developing. Research and learn what may be able to put your business at an advantage. A free giveaway, new store colors, thank you cards for your clientele. It is the small things that add up to the large payoffs.

Offer top quality customer service. Make your customer feel as if they are the only one that matters in the world to you and mean it.

Make your chosen business name flow from your business to your customers lips with ease. Make your business name catchy, or one they can easily remember. Your customers can become your method of promotion. Take the little steps to remind your clientele who you are monthly. Email thoughts of the day, ex. have a gardening business, flower shop? How about sending a garden tip of the month, information about what to plant when? Send monthly emails, start a business newsletter. Provide useful information to your clientele and show you care about them.

When staff is necessary hire quality personnel that reflect positively on you, your passion and who will continually strive to represent you in a positive light.

VALUABLE RESOURCES FOR RUNNING A SMALL BUSINESS

http://www.sba.gov/services/index.html

http://www.businessownersideacafe.com/

http://www.businesstown.com/

http://www.uspto.gov/

http://www.score.org

http://buzgate.org/wa/index.html

http://www.freelancemom.com/

http://www.wholesalecentral.com/Dropshippers.html

http://www.wholesalehub.com/

http://www.ebay.com/

http://www.fastsigns.com/yard-signs.html

http://www.branders.com/

978-0-595-44914-9
0-595-44914-X

www.ingramcontent.com/pod-product-compliance
Lightning Source LLC
Chambersburg PA
CBHW030845180526
45163CB00004B/1452